INVITATIONS

TO

PRAYER

Invitations to Prayer

Selections

from the Writings of

ERIC SYMES ABBOTT

Dean of Westminster,

1959–1974

Printed by
MERIDEN-STINEHOUR PRESS, 1989

Distributor:
FORWARD MOVEMENT PUBLICATIONS
412 Sycamore Street, Cincinnati, Ohio 45202
USA

ISBN 0–88028–098–0

For
AGATHA NORMAN
and the
St. Faith's Fellowship

Eric Abbott shows us the world of sacrament and symbol where everything means more than it means because it is loved by God.
Our prayer at best is our response to that love.

— MADELEINE L'ENGLE

OUR prayer to God is partly articulate, and partly inarticulate. For most of us it is more inarticulate than articulate. I would appeal to the sense of the inarticulate prayer which I believe every human heart is making and which the Holy Spirit of God is seeking to make articulate in us, as more and more a conscious and deliberate faith is formed.

CHRISTIAN prayer is response.
In this it is distinguished from all those
spiritual disciplines and exercises,
however good, which are initiated by
men and women for their own improvement,
for their own purification, for their own
increase of self-control.
The Christian says "we love God because
He first loved us." Our love which
ascends to God is the love
which has first come down from God.

KNOWING that prayer is response
brings us face to face with
the givenness of the Christian life.
It is enormously strengthening,
for the fact that *God is*
is the One Fact that we need
to know for our peace.

ACCEPTING the truth about ourselves
is not agreeable and a strong
resistance is put up by all of us.
We are blind to the truth.
"Lord, that I may receive my sight"
is a good prayer.

S<small>ELF-KNOWLEDGE</small> will include
not only the discovery of our mingled
debit and credit items of character
but also the realization that
this *plus* has made us proud, this *minus*
has made us afraid, this fear has
made us evasive and faithless,
this memory is an unhealed wound
which adds to our guilt.
We need a self-knowledge
which takes account of all the facts
of our life in all its complexity.

BEWARE of thinking that every form of melancholy, indifference, disenchantment is to be identified with wisdom.

L ET us pray that each and all
of us may find our true way,
and that all our knowledge and
all our life may be at the
disposal of the love of God.
And of the love of God,
friendship is sacramental.

It does seem that people
come to themselves when
they are able to repent and
certainly when they are forgiven.
Love when it is true longs
to forgive. Forgiveness does not
mean forgetting; it means
remembering the past in a new way.
When we ask for Christ's forgiveness,
the effect is that in so far as
the past is remembered again,
it will have lost its power to hurt us
and make us afraid.

God's word to individuals and nations
is never a word of judgment *only*.
It is always a double word of judgment
and mercy. Therefore although
we pray for our sins and our follies,
a situation which looks desperate
can be changed, hope can be re-born,
a new direction can be taken and
a big recovery can take place
in a comparatively short time.

We are all persons in the making
and in a real sense we are
making and re-making one another.
But how often personal relationships
are marred by hasty, partial or
over-severe judgments.
We must help one another,
not judge one another, and
we must leave the final judgment
to the Divine Patience.
One of the greatest promises
in the New Testament is that
we are accepted in the Beloved.
Let us try to be the ministers
of acceptance.

THE greatest enemy is
not so much sin but anxiety.
Our Lord does not say
"Why are you sinful?"
but "Why are you afraid?"

THE Incarnation
   The Passion
      The Resurrection
        The Ascension
          The Coming of the Spirit
was in order that
Christ might abide in us now,
and that we might abide in Him.

IT is not usually necessary to do more,
but we can be more.
We can be with Christ where he is.
True practical spirituality
is to be with him where he is.
The preposition *with* is immensely
important in the New Testament.
    We live with him
        suffer with him
        die with him
        are buried with him
        and raised with him
        and glorified with him.
Our task is to realise this conformity
of our lives to the life of Christ
who is in us and with us, and to let it
develop within us as the life and
passion of Jesus developed.

GOD alone teaches to pray.
We must remember this, lest we ask
too much of our human teachers,
ask them for that which in the
nature of things they cannot give.
The real teacher of prayer is
the Holy Spirit of God.

WHATEVER we may say about particular
times and methods of prayer,
this much is essential, that each day
should have some dedicated silence in it.
This is the gift of our time to God.
We are to put ourselves at God's disposal
in the quietness. The prayer
will be dispersed throughout our day,
throughout our activity, but there will be
some dedicated spaces of silence.

O LORD, rescue me from myself
and give me unto Thee.
Take away from me all those
things that draw me from Thee
and give me those things
that lead me to Thee.

THE typical prayer of Christians
is Common Prayer which then informs
our private prayer. It is this way round
and not the other. It is not that
private prayer is primary
which then corporate prayer helps along,
corporate prayer being an
optional extra, more or less helpful.

OUR private prayer is balanced
and completed by the liturgy.
The Church's corporate liturgy
can also present us with problems,
but in the liturgy we are lifted out
of our anxieties about our
private prayer, we pray the prayer
of the whole Church, and the
fundamental symbols are still there,
the Cross, the bread, and the wine,
the sharing, the Body of Christ incarnate,
mystical and eucharistic.

THERE is no perfect Liturgy.
What is both important and essential
is that we should not be
too discouraged, and certainly
that we should not be defeated
either by the imperfections of the
Liturgy itself or by the imperfections
of our own self-offering.
The answer to both forms of
imperfection is the perfection of Christ
and his self-offering
to the Father.

THERE is an aridity of our time
which is due to the atrophy of the
imaginative faculties,
an atrophy related on the one hand
to the loss of the transcendent
and the wholly other,
the truly mysterious; related
on the other hand to the starving
of the unconscious of
its life-sustaining symbols,
images and archetypes.

13ᵗʰ century crucifix from the National Gallery of Umbria, Perugia, Italy.

IT is no accident that the Redeemer's arms are outstretched as they are. This is the length, breadth, depth and height of the love of God.

CHRIST'S whole life and death was
an intercessory act—a work of love
in which He gave Himself *to* God
for others, a work of love in which
He became as an intercessor
a representative,
as an intercessor a mediator,
as an intercessor a priest.

INTERIOR discipline makes us by grace
able to meet and overcome the exigencies
of circumstances brought to us by
people and happenings.
We cannot possibly speak of
the discipline of prayer in terms
of man-made rules. Somehow we have
to enter into the heart and mind and will
of the Praying Christ Himself.
Our discipline of prayer includes
such a close following of our Lord
in His desires that we become interceders.
Where love is, there intercession is.

The Baptist's famous words
"He must increase, I must decrease"
apply to us all through our
Christian life.

As we all suffer in degrees more or less,
what we become in and through the
suffering is vital. Shall we become more
full of love and acceptance,
of compassion with other sufferers,
even more full of a certain kind
of peace and joy? Or shall we become
narrower, more self-enclosed,
more self-pitying?

In the Benedicite, Ananias, Azarias and
Misael, the three holy children,
are bidden to praise and bless the Lord.
Why these three?
Because in the old story they were cast
into the burning fiery furnace
because of their stubborn faith in
the living God. Benedicite has come
down to us as the Song of Unconquerable
Faith which they sang to the Lord
in the furnace of fire.

A CREED is something to live by,
not simply to learn by rote. A creed
is also a summary of faith.
Each clause is a highly concentrated and
highly charged "nucleus" of Christian
thought and belief and experience.
At one moment it means little
or nothing, and at another moment
it can mean everything.
Each of us needs the rest of
the Church to back up our individual
saying of the Creed.
When we are weak, others may be
strong and vice versa.

WHEN prayer fails, some substitute action
takes its place, whether good, bad or
neutral. When prayer fails, we fill in
with activity (which may seem creative
and fruitful). And sometimes we fill in
with activism which then becomes
the dominant attitude
and true prayer is crowded out.

THERE is no dichotomy between
prayer and action. Prayer is the time
God uses to love and reincarnate
himself in us, and activity is
the normal expression of this love.
God loves in us,
and others through us.

THE search for meaning has
to be made in the to*ing* and fro*ing*
between a person and whatever
he has to do.

THE life of prayer needs constant
renewal and fresh stimulus.
The factor of rest is related not only
and most obviously to physical
health, but to self-control
and charity. If we are exhausted,
though we may not break down
physically, charity often becomes
a casualty. Rest as described
in the Epistle to the Hebrews
is understood in terms of
activity without friction.

We are faced by griefs and sorrows
and injustices and inequalities
and unfairness which are a moral
as well as an intellectual challenge.
What is to be our reaction?
Fatalism? Stoical endurance?
Mere passivity?
Or that kind of acceptance
of suffering which we see in the Cross,
a bearing of it which exhausts
the power of evil and, by taking the
suffering and the sin in
the suffering, also takes it away?

THE orders in Christ's Church are interdependent. Not the least glory both of the laity and of the ordained priesthood is that each should minister to and strengthen the other. The ministries of the one and of the other are meant to become a creative partnership, under the guidance and enablement of the Holy Spirit, extending into the world the one fontal priesthood which is that of Jesus the High Priest of us all.

In the Old and New Testaments,
the transfiguration of Israel,
of the Church, of the world,
of the Cosmos, is the work
of God the Holy Spirit
in the often intractable material
which is our human nature.

THE Transfiguration was an experience
shared with the disciples. Christ took them
with Him, and His transfiguration was
the first movement towards the disciples'
transfiguration as well.
If we see Him transfigured
we are in a measure transfigured.
We see Him as He is; we see ourselves
in Him. As we begin to contemplate Him,
we begin to be like Him.
Jesus makes Peter, James and John
to be "eyewitnesses of his majesty".
We are all made for that sight.

WE are tempted to think that the chief
Christian sufferings should be those
inflicted by the world upon the Church,
as we rather naively think,
by the "wicked" upon the "good".
Those sufferings however are easy to bear
compared with the peculiar sufferings
we bear as Christians within the Church.
The Church is where the tensions
of human life have to be confronted on
the deepest level.

How can I love my neighbor as myself
when I need him as my enemy—
when I see in him the self I fear to own
and cannot love?

How can there be peace on earth
while our hostilities are our most
cherished possessions—
defining our identity, confirming
our innocence?

LET us go on together
even if the way be dark.

WHEN we come to the end, let us
commend our spirits to God
our Creator and redeemer in faith,
believing that he who raised
Jesus from the dead will be able
to take what we have done
for him, whether explicitly or
implicitly, and will gather
it into his Kingdom,
to be in that Kingdom that
particular enrichment of the
Kingdom's glory which our
particular life had to contribute.
For there is something
which only you can bring
into the Kingdom of God.

THE quintessence of the prayer of the
whole body of Christians, and of
Christ in his members are these words
from the liturgy:

Lift up your hearts
　　We lift them up unto the Lord.
Let us give thanks unto our Lord God.
　　It is meet and right so to do.
It is very meet, right and our bounden
　　duty that we should at all times
　　and in all places give thanks unto
　　Thee, O Lord, Holy Father,
　　Almighty, Everlasting God.
Therefore with angels and archangels
　　and with all the company of heaven
　　we laud and magnify Thy glorious name;
　　evermore praising Thee and saying
Holy, Holy, Holy, Lord God of Hosts,
　　Heaven and earth are full of Thy glory.
　　Glory be to Thee, O Lord Most High.
　　Amen.

REFERENCES

PAGE   SOURCE

9   The Dean's Installation Service, 30 November 1959.

11   Vaughan Memorial Lecture, "Education in the
        Spiritual Life", Doncaster Grammar School, 1961.

13   *Escape or Freedom*, p. 10, W. Heffner & Sons Ltd.,
        Cambridge, 1939.

15   St. Faith's Fellowship School of Prayer, 22 February
        1962.

17   Undated talk on *Penitence*.

19   Lent Course II, 1965.

21   Service of Dedication of the Academic Year,
        The University Church of St. Mary the Virgin,
        Oxford, 12 October 1958.

23   Lent Course IV, 8 March 1961.

25   Westminster Abbey Community Association, 1969.

27   St. Faith's Fellowship School of Prayer, 1968.

29   St. Faith's Fellowship School of Prayer, 22 February
        1962.

31   Easter, undated.

33   Lent Course, 1965.

35   Sermon on the BBC Home Service, 14 September
        1947.

REFERENCES

References

PAGE   SOURCE

67   St. Faith's Fellowship School of Prayer, 29 October
        1968.

69   Retreat Notes, Pleshey, 1–4 October 1965.

71   "Discipline in Prayer", 17 November 1966,
        and St. Faith's Fellowship, 30 October 1973.

73   St. Faith's Fellowship Lent Course, 1970.

75   St. Faith's Fellowship School of Prayer, 14 February
        1967.

77   "The Spirit and the Church", Wednesdays in July,
        St. Margaret's Church, July, 1973.

79   Transfiguration Retreat, Pleshey, 13–16 September,
        1946, and Lent Course IV, 1965.

81   Broadcast from the Chapel of King's College, London,
        20 March 1955.

83   Christmas Day in the Abbey, 1969.

85   Sunday Evening in the Abbey, Palm Sunday, 22 March
        1970.

87   *The Compassion of God and the Passion of Christ*, p. 95,
        Geoffrey Bles Ltd., London, 1963.

89   Sermon on the BBC Home Service, 28 September
        1947.

ERIC SYMES ABBOTT, KCVO, DD

1906	Born in Nottingham, England 26 May, son of William Henry and Mary Abbott
	Educated at Nottingham High School Jesus College, Cambridge Westcott House, Cambridge
1930	Ordained Deacon in St. Paul's Cathedral, London, to serve as curate of St. John the Evangelist, Smith Square, Westminster
1931	Ordained priest
1932–1936	Chaplain of King's College, London
1934–1936	Chaplain of King's College Theological Hostel
1936–1945	Warden of Lincoln Theological College
1940–1960	Canon and Prebendary of Sancta Crucis in Lincoln Cathedral
1945–1955	Dean of King's College, London
1948–1952	Chaplain to HM the King
1952–1959	Chaplain to HM the Queen
1952–1959	Warden of Keble College, Oxford
1959–1974	Dean of Westminster
1966	Knight Commander of the Victorian Order
1974	Retired to live in Vincent Square, Westminster
1983	Died in Guildford 6 June

Compiled by
PEGGY CHISHOLM

Designed by
THOMAS GODDARD

Photograph by
LILLIAN RAY

Printed by
MERIDEN-STINEHOUR PRESS

Typeface
BASKERVILLE

Paper
MONADNOCK TEXT, (Sub 80)